Amusements for adults included optical 'toys' based on the persistence of vision; the Phenakistoscope of around 1840 (sitting next to the sewing machine) was invented in 1832; the Zoetrope (bottom right) with its picture strip was invented in 1834 but not produced until 1867, and the Praxinoscope with candle and shade was patented in 1877. The stereoscopic viewer (under the aspidistra, left) gave a three-dimensional view of a photograph. Mechanical music became continuous with the Orguinette in 1880 (see opposite) and then in the 1890s, the first talking machine, Edison's Phonograph, using a cylindrical disc, and the gramophone with its flat disc. The Gower-Bell telephone from around 1895 (centre) had two ear pieces. The Daily Mail celebrated the dawn of the new century on 31st Dec 19..

1848, Queen Victoria with Albert and six of their eventual nine children.

INTRODUCTION

When Queen Victoria came to the throne in 1837, it was the beginning of a reign that would see immense change - in lifestyle as well as in economic progress. The industrial revolution was well underway, with the population moving towards the towns and cities to man the great factories. Heavy transport was moving from the canals to the railways, and it was the railways that offered ordinary people the chance of going to the seaside. Communication improved with the introduction of the uniform penny post in 1840; the telegram service had been developing during the 1840s and 1850s (but messages often contained bad news: top left, 1860); the telephone, which had been invented in 1878, was still only for the rich, and for some businesses by the 1890s.

Many Acts of Parliament were passed to improve health and education and the conditions of factory workers. Charities helped the poor, but there was still great hardship. The co-operative movement for workers began in 1844 when a grocer's shop opened for weavers in the mill town of Rochdale. A fairer system of voting for members of Parliament gradually developed, and trade unions grew in strength, so that by the end of the century a quarter of all those in work were members of a union.

The constant fear of infection, heightened by outbreaks of cholera, tuberculosis and typhoid (from which Prince Albert died in 1861) led to a great regard for hygiene and sanitation, and the use of antiseptics and disinfectants during the 1890s, made by Jeyes, Izal and Lever with Lifebuoy soap. A better system of water distribution and sewers, together with a wider use of water closets, helped to improve living conditions. During the second half of the century, the population doubled to nearly 40 million.

Above all, the end of the Victorian era saw many innovations. Electric lighting in streets from 1881, in homes during the 1890s. Typewriters (here in art nouveau style) enabled women to find a foothold in the business world. Mid-1890s saw motor cars emerge - by 1900 there were some 750 on the roads of Britain. From 1890 comics for children, such as Comic Cuts and Illustrated Chips were available for a halfpenny.

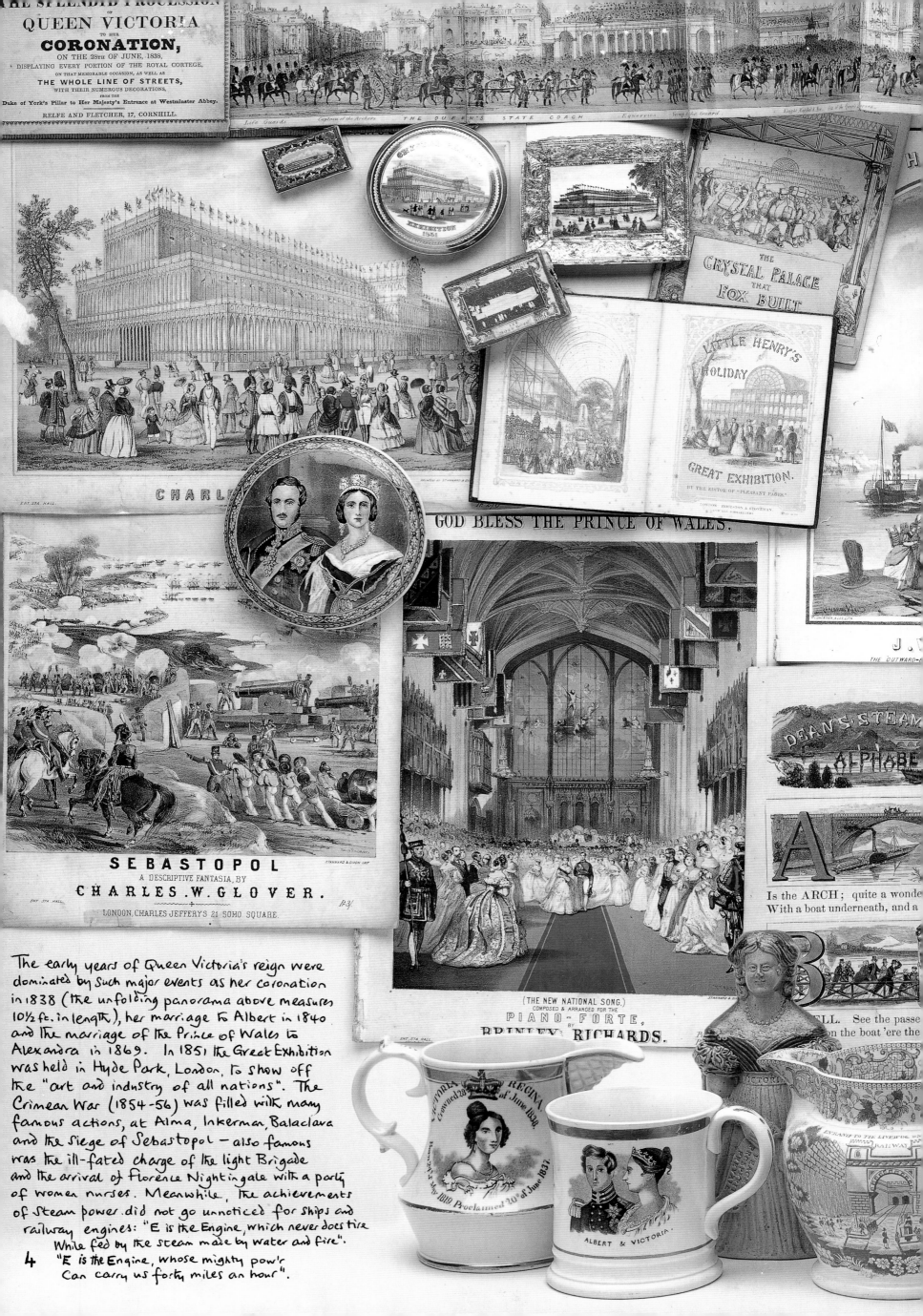

THE SPLENDID PROCESSION
OF
QUEEN VICTORIA
TO HER
CORONATION,
ON THE 28TH OF JUNE, 1838,
DISPLAYING EVERY PORTION OF THE ROYAL CORTEGE,
ON THAT MEMORABLE OCCASION, AS WELL AS
THE WHOLE LINE OF STREETS,
WITH THEIR NUMEROUS DECORATIONS,
FROM THE
Duke of York's Pillar to Her Majesty's Entrance at Westminster Abbey.
RELFE AND FLETCHER, 17, CORNHILL.

THE
CRYSTAL PALACE
THAT
FOX BUILT

LITTLE HENRY'S
HOLIDAY
AT THE
GREAT EXHIBITION.
BY THE EDITOR OF "PLEASANT PAGES."

GOD BLESS THE PRINCE OF WALES,

DEAN'S STEAM
ALPHABE

A
Is the ARCH; quite a wonde
With a boat underneath, and a

SEBASTOPOL
A DESCRIPTIVE FANTASIA, BY
CHARLES. W. GLOVER.
LONDON, CHARLES JEFFERYS 21 SOHO SQUARE.

(THE NEW NATIONAL SONG.)
COMPOSED & ARRANGED FOR THE
PIANO-FORTE,
BY
BRINLEY RICHARDS.

The early years of Queen Victoria's reign were dominated by such major events as her coronation in 1838 (the unfolding panorama above measures 10½ ft. in length), her marriage to Albert in 1840 and the marriage of the Prince of Wales to Alexandra in 1869. In 1851 the Great Exhibition was held in Hyde Park, London, to show off the "art and industry of all nations". The Crimean War (1854-56) was filled with many famous actions, at Alma, Inkerman, Balaclava and the siege of Sebastopol — also famous was the ill-fated charge of the light Brigade and the arrival of Florence Nightingale with a party of women nurses. Meanwhile, the achievements of steam power did not go unnoticed for ships and railway engines: "E is the Engine, which never does tire While fed by the steam made by water and fire".

4 "E is the Engine, whose mighty pow'r Can carry us forty miles an hour".

THE GREAT EASTERN.—Named "THE LEVIATHAN," Nov. 3rd, 1857.

LENGTH, 691 Feet. BREADTH, 118 Feet. TONNAGE, 22500 Tons.

Is the CAPTAIN; above us he stands,
Directing the steersman by moving his hands.

Is the DECK, swept so nice and so clean,
On which very often may dancing be seen.

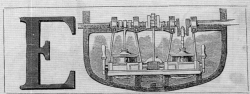

Is the ENGINE, which never does tire,
While fed by the steam made by water and fire.

E is the Engine, whose mighty pow'r
Can carry us forty miles an hour.

F is the Fire, the best *slave* we know;
But, once our master, the direst foe.

G is the Guard, taking care of all,
And watching lest harm the train befall.

H is the Horse-h... which ...lers need,
Who carry by tra... a gallan...

CHARGE OF THE SCOTS GREYS AT BALACLAVA

BATTLE of INKERMAN

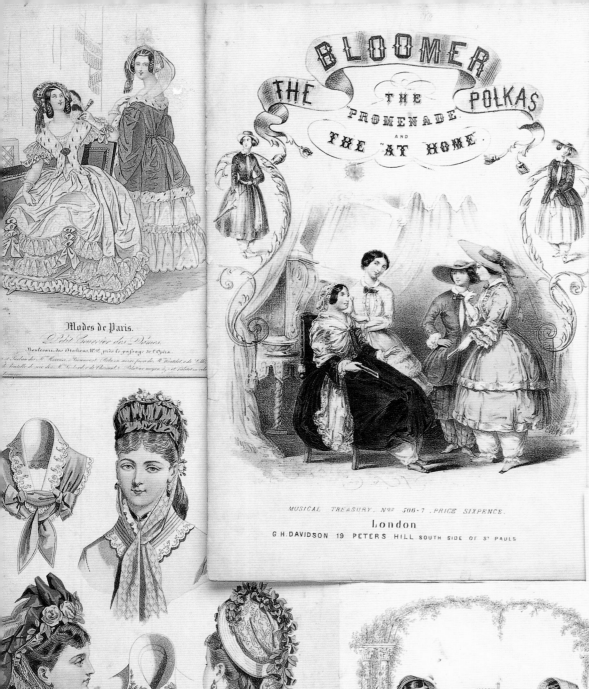

Modes de Paris.
Petit Courrier des Dames.

THE MILLINER & DRESSMAKER
AND
WAREHOUSEMAN'S GAZETTE.

THE
BLOOMER
POLKAS
THE "PROMENADE" AND THE "AT HOME."

MUSICAL TREASURY. Nᵒˢ 506-7. PRICE SIXPENCE.
London
G.H.DAVIDSON 19 PETERS HILL SOUTH SIDE OF Sᵗ PAULS

WHAT OUR SWELLS ARE COMING TO!

TO MISS BELLA MOORE.
GRECIAN BEND
QUADRILLE.

THE WORLD OF FASHION.

NIGHT
PATENT DR...

Society women needed to be seen in the latest Paris fashions, which constantly changed. Designs were illustrated in the fashion periodicals like The Young Ladies Journal. In the 1840s ladies wore full skirts with as many as six petticoats. "Bloomers" were introduced from America in 1851, at the same time as the Singer sewing machine. The fashion for crinoline skirts, supported on wire cages, started in the mid-fifties and lasted about 20 years. The bustle was in vogue from 1870 till about 1890. In the 1890s a more slender silhouette became fashionable. A corset was necessary to keep most figures in shape. The 'wasp-waist' of the mid-1890s balanced the exaggerated 'leg-of-mutton' puffed sleeves.

Gentlemen could be as colourful as women, and called 'dandies' or 'swells'. The top hat arrived in 1797; the bowler from 1849.

May 1858. THE WORLD OF FASHION.

THE
YOUNG LADIES JOURNAL
ALBUM
Nᵒ 152 OF THE LATEST PARIS FASHION

OH! THAT TOP HAT

Theatre and Music Hall Rights Reserved.

SUNG BY FRANK CO

Copyright

LONDON: B. FELDMAN & Co 9, BERNER

MAYPOLE SOAP DYES ANY COLOUR

VISITOR: "HOW LOVELY! WHY MAUD, HOW DID YOU MANAGE IT ALL?"
MAUD: "EASILY ENOUGH, THESE BLOUSES, UNDERSKIRT, RIBBONS, CUSHION COVERS, IN FACT, EVERYTHING IN THIS ROOM IS DYED WITH THAT WONDERFUL PREPARATION MAYPOLE SOAP."

THE "VERY THING" FOR LADIES
FOR AN ELEGANT FIGURE & GOOD HEALTH
HARNESS' ELECTRIC CORSE
PRICE ONLY 5/6 POST FREE.

MAYPOLE SOAP DYES ANY COLOR

Won't Wash-out or Fade

THE **Y & N.** PATENT DIAGONAL SEAM **CORSETS.**
THREE OLD MEDALS.

ALL IN SEARCH OF HEALTH
Should Wear Harness'
"ELECTROPATHIC BELT.
FOR SUFFE MEN & WO
FOR NERVOUS EXHAUSTION, NEURALGIA, RHEUMATISM, INDIGESTIO SLEEPLESSNESS, LADIES' AILMENTS IT IMPARTS NEW LIFE AND VIGOU

10/6 Allen Foster & Co 10/6
A Costume for 10/6
THE LONDON MANUFACTURERS
THE HALF GUINEA COSTUME OF THE DAY.
UTTERLY UNRIVALLED ALL THE WORLD OVER

WHAT ANOTHER NEW HAT?

SEE OVER.

Lanoline Soap, Cold Cream, & Pomade
Toilet Lanoline
For the health and beauty of the skin and hair
(OVER)

WELDON'S ILLUSTRATED DRESSMAKER
A Paper pattern and Coloured plate presented with every number.
CHRISTMAS DOUBLE NUMBER

WELDON'S FASHIONS FOR DECEMBE
Flat patterns of Costumes 6ᵈ each, untrimmed 9
DESIGNED BY WELDONS, LIMITED FASHION PUBLISHERS, 30 & 31. SOUTHAMPTON STREET, STRAND, LOND

THE YOUNG LADIES JOURNAL MONTHLY PANORAMA OF FASHION
D. NICHOLSON & COMPY 50.51 52 AND 53 ST PAULS CHURCHYARD & 66 PATERNOSTER ROW CORNER OF CHEAPSIDE LONDON SILK MERCERS TO THE QUEEN
& Outfitters to all parts of the World supply all the Goods represented in the Above Illustrations and from Whom prices and particulars may be had gratis upon application
1000 PATTERNS OF NEWEST SILKS AND DRESS MATERIALS ALSO SENT POST FREE

Published with the YOUNG LADIES JOURNAL
MAY PART 1880

ION PLATES OF 20 FIGURES
5 CHILDREN'S Fashions

7

JUST AS YOU ARE FOR NINEPENCE
OR THE ART PHOTOGRAPHER,

COMIC SONG
WRITTEN & COMPOSED BY   & SUNG WITH IMMENSE SUCCESS BY
T. S. LONSDALE.   HENRI CLARK.
LONDON: CHARLES SHEARD, 192 HIGH HOLBORN. W.C.

Magnificent photograph albums of family members were proudly kept by many households during the 1880s and 1890s. The photographic process had started in the 1830s, becoming commercially successful during the 1840s with studio photographs taken on the Daguerreotype camera. Here was a cheap alternative to the painted portrait. Indeed, by the 1890s many people were taking pictures themselves with cameras such as George Eastman's Kodak (available originally as a camera for detectives in 1888), and being encouraged by journals like the Amateur Photographer launched in 1884.

9

Although many newspapers had been established for some time (The Times in 1788), it was the railways that enabled their wider and more rapid distribution, along with an increasing range of publications. Punch was launched in 1841 and in 1867 was imitated by Judy introducing the comic character Ally Sloper (who later appeared in his own Half Holiday from 1884). The Illustrated News was launched in 1843 and in 1891 The Strand Magazine arrived with its Sherlock Holmes stories. In 1848 W.H.Smith began to set up a chain of bookstalls at railway stations, which numbered some 1200 by the 1890s. Many publications used similar names — the Manchester Guardian was launched in 1855, a rival to The Guardian already established (note the traditional mourning livery of black borders, this time for Prince Albert's death in 1861) The Daily Mail was launched in 1896 and Daily Express in 1900.

THE "WELCOME PACKET" HORNIMAN'S TEA.

LONDON: S. W. PARTRIDGE & CO., 9, PATERNOSTER ROW.

After the picture by Joseph Clark in the Royal Academy.

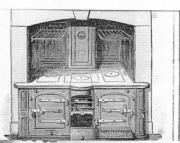

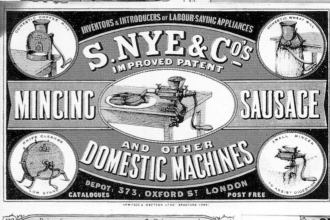

Working class homes were sparsely decorated with
the bare essentials of domestic comfort. For
the more affluent there were the benefits of
household innovations – the gas cooker, clothes
washer, sewing machine and carpet sweeper.
Decorative tiles brightened up the fireplace
or house doorway; and linoleum, invented in
the 1860s, provided a cheaper, highly durable
and easily cleaned form of floor covering,
which could be bought in a variety
of patterns that would "never wear out".

12

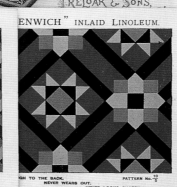

PATENT OIL WARMING STOVES
THE BEST IN THE WORLD

A great variety of candles were available for many uses - lighting at dinner table, night lights, piano candles, ballroom candles, carriage candles and food warmers. Candle power was the principal source of light along with the more expensive lamp oil, which was improved when paraffin oil became more efficiently used in the 1880s. Gas lighting was well advanced by the 1870s, though not widely used, but that changed with the arrival of the incandescent gas mantle in 1891 - then the electric light gradually started to compete. Rippingille's world renowned oil warming stoves were used to warm any room, including bathroom, landing, hall or greenhouse.

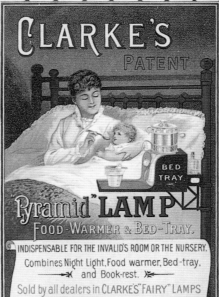

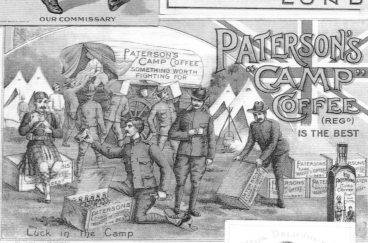
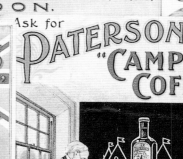

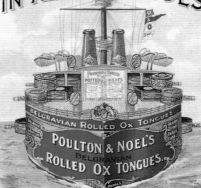

So many new brands arrived in the grocers' shops during the 1880s and 1890s, that the merits of each new arrival had to be extolled. Colourful posters appeared on the hoardings erected in towns and cities, and miniature poster adverts (as shown here) were inserted into the growing number of magazines. The grocer would hand out samples and paper novelties, such as those below – that for Paysandu Ox Tongues shows the latest in motor travel – and many of these ended up pasted into children's scrapbooks.

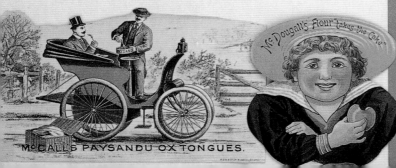
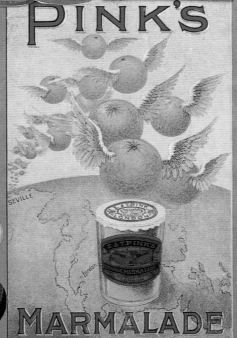
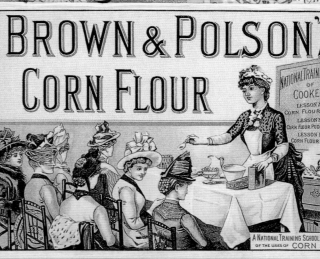

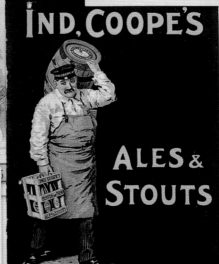

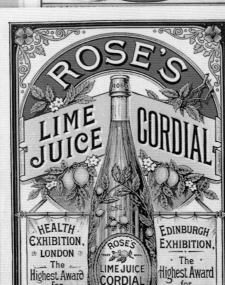
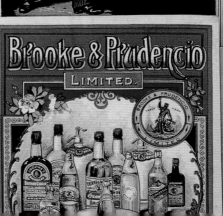

During the second half of the nineteenth century, more brands were filling the shelves of the grocers' stores – sauces, pickles and relishes, mustard, potted meats, baking powder and an increasing variety of canned foods. Bovril was launched in 1886, Cerebos Salt in 1894 and Lyle's Golden Syrup in 1885. By 1900 many of the commodities traditionally purchased in bulk by the grocer (which he then weighed out and wrapped to each customer's requirements) were now being done by the manufacturer in pre-weighed sealed packs "untouched by hand". Tea, coffee, cocoa, flour and spices could all be found in small individual pre-wrapped amounts. Most biscuits, though, were sold loose from large 7lb tins. The 'fancy' biscuit began to appear in the 1840s: Huntley & Palmers were formed in 1841 (the distinctive 'garter and buckle' design for their labels came out in 1851); Peek, Frean & Co were founded in 1857; and in

1851 Jacobs moved on to baking fancy biscuits, with their Cream Crackers arriving in 1885. Jam was mostly made at home, but a widening choice of 'shop bought' jams were becoming available; Keillers marmalade began in 1797, while Robertson's started to manufacture in the 1860s. Bottled beers had come into use during the 1840s, the Bass beer label being designed in 1855. The Hamilton type bottle for aerated waters had been in use since 1814 — it had a 'pointed' end and thus it lay on its side and kept the cork moist, once opened it could be placed in a special holder. Many of the shoe blacking labels date back to the 1820s and 1830s; those for knife polish date from the 1850s onwards. The dry soap manufacturer of Hudson had been established since 1843, but the new soap launched by Lever in 1885 was Sunlight Soap, followed in 1894 by Lifebuoy Soap. Robin Starch arrived in 1899 to join the many other starch brands on the market.

19

CALVERT'S
Nº5 CARBOLIC SOAP

CALVERT'S
Nº5 CARBOLIC SOAP

Disinfects
An Excellent
Skin Soap

F.C.CALVERT & Cº
MANCHESTER ENGLAND.

Sunlight Soap

Makes Clothes Sweet & Clean.

Makes Clothes White
Makes Hearts Light

THOUSANDS OF HOMES ARE BRIGHTENED
BY THE DAILY USE OF

THE GREAT DIRT EXTRACTOR
BORAX
EXTRACT OF SOAP

Appointed by
Special Royal Warrant
Makers to
Her Majesty the Queen

BORAX EXTRACT OF SOAP
WHICH FOR ALL WASHING, CLEANING AND PURIFYING
PURPOSES IS SIMPLY PERFECTION!
ALL GROCERS SELL IT IN ¼-LB. PACKETS, DOZEN & HALF-DOZEN PARCELS

PATENT BORAX CO., LTD., SOLE MAKERS, WORKS, LADYWOOD, BIRMINGHAM, LONDON

OAKEY'S Wellington Knife Polish
OAKEY'S Black Lead

A MINISTERING ANGEL

BOVRIL

Liebig COMPANY
Peptone of B

A highly NOURISHING & PALATABLE
For INVALIDS & CONVALES

Sutherland Bra
ENGLISH

PRESERVED PROVISION
Prepared by
J. & A. CARPENTER   Sutherland
London

Liebig "COMPANY'S" Extract of Beef
FINEST MEAT FLAVOURING STOCK
FOR SOUPS SAUCES AND MADE DISHES

use BORWICK'S
BAKING
POWDER
It is the Best
For Bread
Cakes &
Pastry

BORWICKS
Baking
Powder
Is the best
that MONEY
can buy

For Bread
Cake
Pastry

RIZINE PRODUCTS
WHAT THEY ARE AND HOW TO USE THEM

FIRST EDITION
1·000·000
RIZINE WORKS.
87 Borough High St. LONDON SE

STEPHENSON BROS' SUPERIOR
- NON-MERCURIAL
PLATE POWDER.

LIEBIG COMPANY'S
PRACTICAL COOKERY BOOK

BORAX
STARCH &c.

JEYES' DISINFECTANTS.
64. CANNON St LONDON.

Liebig COMPANY'S EXTRACT OF MEAT
Then STOCKPOT for Soups. Made dishes. Sauces.
Meat. Game and Fish.

DOMESTIC SERVANTS'
COTTON WASHING DRESSES.
FOR HOUSEMAIDS, NURSES, Etc.

Are the speciality of The Daughters of the Deep Sea.
GORLESTON. SUFFOLK.

For Spring Clean
USE
CALVERT

Nº 5
CARBOLIC SOAP
F.C CALVERT & Cº MANCHESTER ENG

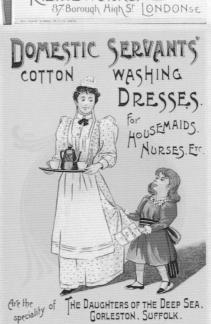

* For Washing, Cleaning & Scouring Ever

The Wily Policeman
MADE WITH
COOMBS' EUREKA PASTRY FLOUR
"EUREKA"

BORAX DRY SOAP
USED IN THE CASTLE & IN THE COTTAGE

THE KITCHEN.

SHOULD ALWAYS BE USED
FOR WASHING
Clothes, Linen, Hands,
Glass, Earthenware,
and Everything;
Cleaning Paint,
Scouring Floors, &c.

HUDSON'S
Extract
Of Soap

LATHERS
FREELY
SOFTENS
WATER

For Scouring Floors,
Greasy Woodwork, &c.

For Washing Dishes,
Plates, China, Glass, &c.

Sold by all Grocers,
Oilmen, &c.

SUNLIGHT
SOAP

LEA & PERRINS' SAUCE

THE BELVEDERE LODGE
LAUNDRY

SAMPLE POST FREE
ON RECEIPT OF
4ª in STAMPS.

PASCALL'S
PORTABLE

FROM THE GLEN LAUND

The grander the house, the more servants would be employed – the housekeeper, lady's maid, cook, nurse and housemaid through to the butler, valet and footman – each with his or her duties around the home; whether cleaning, cooking or polishing, all would sing the praises of Hudson's Dry Soap. A boon to many servants were the products to make life 'below stairs' that bit easier – Oakey's knife polish, Stevenson's plate powder, Calvert's carbolic soap, Liebigs Extract of Meat, Pascall's portable jellies and blanc-manges.

For the genteel classes, and thus those who could afford them, the use of perfumes and toiletries was increasingly in evidence as the choice extended. Toothpowder and dentifrices were seen as a luxury by the majority, who would use a cheap alternative abrasive like salt or often soot. However, some toilet soaps were becoming popular amongst the middle classes by the 1880s, such as Pears' Soap which was widely promoted. Millais' painting 'Bubbles' of 1886 was later purchased to promote Pears'; the society actress, Lillie Langtry, endorsed Pears': "For years I have used your soap, and no other"; and in 1891 the Pears' Annual began, giving away colourful prints.

"ARGOSY" CIGARETTES.

Manufactured by

W. & F. FAULKNER, L^TD

BLACKFRIARS ROAD. LONDON.

The smoking of tobacco in a pipe grew throughout the Victorian reign, but the relatively expensive cigarette was greatly reduced in price when the Bonsack machine was introduced in 1888, and Wills' Wild Woodbine and Cinderella cigarettes were sold at five for a penny. Although women were often featured in the advertisements, they rarely smoked – except to make an effect; yet the liberated woman could hold her own at the helm (as above, late 1890s). Friction matches had been in existence since the 1830s, with Bryant & May (established 1851) being the dominant manufacturer.

ALL THE WAY.

This Song may be Sung in Public without fee or Licence, Except at Music Halls & Theatres.

Written by
HARRY DACRE AND **CHAS. DEANE.**

Composed and Sung by
CHARLES DEANE.

THE SUCCESS OF THE SEASON
FELDMAN'S FIRST COMIC ANNUAL

CHELSEA. STRAND AND PICCADILLY CIRCUS
BANK LUDGATE HILL
(ANE ST KNIGHTSBRIDGE & BROMPTON)
PIMLICO

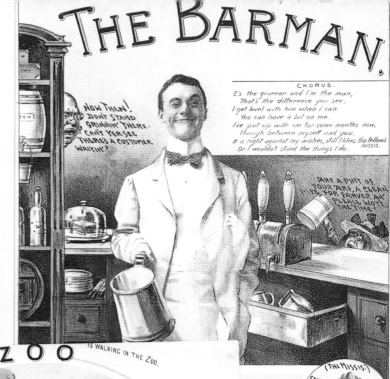

THE BARMAN.

CHORUS.
'E's the govenor and I'm the man,
That's the difference you see.
I get level with him when I can.
You can have a bit on me
I've put up with 'im for some months now,
though between myself and you,
It is right against my wishes, still I likes the fellow
Or I wouldn't stand the things I do.

NOW THEN! DON'T STAND GRINNIN' THERE
CAN'T YER SEE THERE'S A COSTOMER WAITIN'?

ARF A PINT OF FOUR 'ARF, A CLEAN GLASS FOR FARVER, AN' TELL 'IM WOT'S THE TIME MISSIS

ZOO

The O.K. thing on Sunday ____ is walking in the Zoo.

GRAND CHORUS.

TOO LATE!!!

GALOP
BY
FELIX HUNT

COME & HELP ME DO THE CELLAR WORK WILKINS (THE MISSIS)

FIRE BRIGA

EO,
s by
RD.

THE S

JEMMY RIDDLE.

HOT EEL PIES

His name was Jemmy Riddle and he play'd upon the Fiddle.
And he managed for to diddle me of my true love

Written & Composed by
C.W. HUNT.

Sung by
FRED FRENCH.

LONDON, H.D'ALCORN & Co 8, RATHBONE PLACE, W. & 351 OXFORD St W.

CLARA CUMMINGS BORN AT CHATHAM,

ALSOPP'S BITTER BEER.

BAR

LONDON CHATHAM & DOVER RAILWAY TIME TABLES SOLD HERE

COMPOSED
AND SUNG WITH IMMENSE SUCCESS
WRITTEN EXPRESSLY FOR HIM
E. W. MACKNEY,
G. H. GEORGE.

LONDON, B. WILLIAMS, 11, PATERNOSTER ROW

Pr. 2/6

CHA

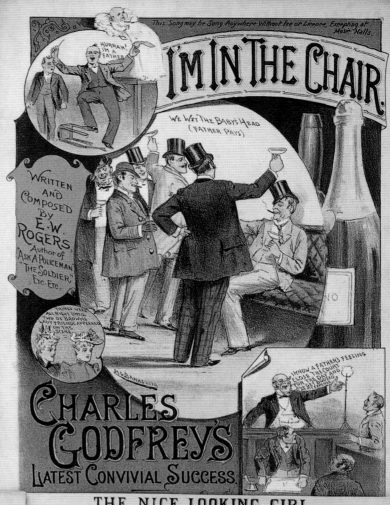

Before the coming of the phonograph or record player in the 1890s, most music was played 'live', mainly on the piano from sheet music – for listening or dancing. Polite society deemed it necessary for young ladies, in particular, to play the piano and sing – all part of Victorian entertainment, and the courting scene. The lower classes found their entertainment in the music halls, where comedians performed and sang comic songs which reflected the topics of the day. George Robey arrived in 1891.

Sticking scraps into special scrap albums was a peculiarly Victorian pastime. The development of colour printing, and die-cut and embossing techniques, produced the glorious results seen here from the 1890s. Children were encouraged to make scrap albums (see above), sticking each item in with glue from a huge pot. Hundreds of different subjects were covered, from floral bouquets (pp 30-31) to royal 'relief scraps' (pp 52-53) and Christmas scenes (p 51).

Welcome
Old Friends
and
New.

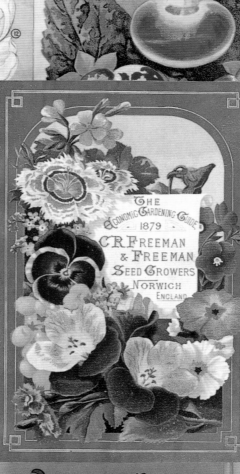
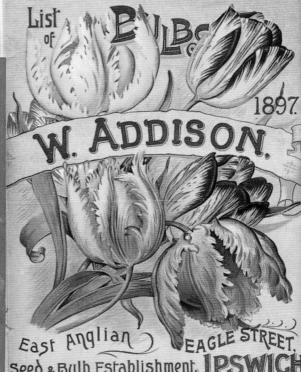

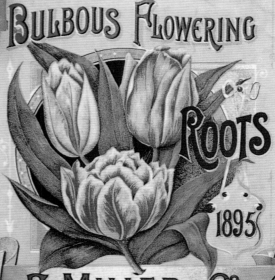

CLAY'S FERTILIZER

RENOWNED PLANT FOOD

'S A.1. POWDER
D KILLER

PATENT
EXCELSIOR

Horse Lawn Mower

GARDENERS'
Calendar & Guide
EDITED BY
Carl Owen Greening
92 LONG ACRE

PURE
ICHTHEMIC
GUANO
FERTILIZES THE WORLD.
TWENTY AWARDS OF MERIT.
The genuine bears Registered Trade Mark and name—
WM. COLCHESTER, IPSWICH.
Packets, 1lb., 6d. 2 lbs., 1/- 7 lbs., 2/6.
Postage extra.
Bags, 14 lbs., 4/6 ; 28 lbs., 7/6 ;
56 lbs., 12/6 ;
112 lbs., 20/—Carriage paid.

"EUREKA"
Weed Killer.

"Bless my soul, not a
weed to be seen"

REGISTERED

"USE"
CLAY'S FERTILIZER
IT IS A PLANT FOOD

A HIGHLY
CONCENTRATED
MANURE
For VINES, ROSES
CHRYSANTHEMUMS
CUCUMBERS
TOMATOES
AND ALL HORTICULTURAL PURPOSES.
INVALUABLE AS A LAWN DRESSING.

SUTTON'S
UNADULTERATED

SUTTON'S ENGLISH SEEDS
FOR ALL PARTS OF THE WORLD

GRASS SEEDS
IN USE
THROUGHOUT THE WORLD

SUTTON & SONS

JOHN CROWLEY & CO. SHEFFIELD
SOLE MANUFACTURERS OF
The
INVINCIBLE First Prize
GOLD MEDAL
LAWN MOWER
NATIONAL
LAWN MOWER
CONTEST

SUTTON'S
AMATEUR'S GUIDE
IN
HORTICULTURE
1879
SUTTON & SONS,
THE QUEEN'S SEEDSMEN,
READING.

1893.
Spring
Catalogue
of
SEEDS
THOMAS PERKINS & SONS,
Seed Merchants
and Nurserymen,
34 DRAPERY, NORTHAMPTON.

Price of Seed
per packet
2 s. 6 d.
For description &c
See other side.

FLOWER SHOW

THE AUTOMATON LAWN MOWER

DESIGNED AND MANUFACTURED BY
RANSOMES, SIMS & HEAD,
ORWELL WORKS, IPSWICH.

THEY ARE EXTREMELY SIMPLE, VERY DURABLE, LIGHT IN DRAUGHT,
AND NOT LIABLE TO GET OUT OF ORDER.
MORE THAN 2400 AUTOMATON LAWN MOWERS
ARE GIVING THE GREATEST SATISFACTION.

RANSOMES
LAWN MOWERS
THE BEST IN THE WORLD

ASTERS Pæony-Flowered

BROS. NORWICH.

VALSE
BY
CHARLES COOTE Jr

During the 1870s and 1880s, the middle
classes increasingly became proud home
owners, and their gardens also received
lavish attention. The more adventurous
grew a wide variety of vegetables:
asparagus, artichokes, broccoli,
celery, cucumber, radishes, leeks
and lettuce. But the greatest effort
went into the flowers, when gardeners'
blooms vied with each other at
flower shows and horticultural society
meetings. The RHS had been established
since 1804. As the towns and cities
prospered, they were able to afford
municipal parks where the public
could enjoy the well laid out beds
full of brilliant flowers (children's
playgrounds were opening – the first in
Manchester 1859).

A DISSECTED MAP OF THE WORLD.

Canoeing in the open Water.

Just in Time.

Putting Provisions on Board a Kayak.

RAILWAY SCENES.

PEACOCK'S DOUBLE DIS...

GEOG...

AUS...

SPOONER'S PICTURE O...

Leopard

SUPERIOR DISSECTED MAPS

STH. AMERICA

SP...

WILD...

One of the most popular pastimes for children was the dissected puzzle (known as a jigsaw puzzle after the mechanical fretsaw or jigsaw was introduced in the 1870s). They were used at first more as an educational toy to instruct children in geography (pieces being cut to the shape of a country or a county), or as a Sunday School amusement with biblical references. The earliest dissected puzzles date from the 1760s; the puzzle of the "railway scene" depicts a railway engine of the 1850s with an inset of James Watt who had greatly improved the efficiency of the steam engine in 1769.

While wooden toys for children were common all through Victoria's reign, ranging from cheap tops to the more intricate boats and traditional Noah's Ark for Sundays, the manufacture of tin toys had become widespread by the 1870s. Board games had been favoured since before 1800 for family entertainment; the new amusement of the 1890s was the game of snakes and ladders, which came from India. The magic lantern projectors (opposite, far right) imitated their adult counterparts. The galloping gig (below) was the most luxurious of push-chairs, as the two horses pranced alternately when pushed. In 1893 William Britain began to make toy soldiers from lead, using hollow casting - metal toy soldiers had been 'flat' previously.

PUSSIES PARTY.

A family cat, with wealth and all that,
Had three daughters handsome and hearty;
"Come, let's enjoy life," said his purring youn...
"Invite a few friends to a .party."
So he sat down to write invitations polite
To those whom he wished...

Some cats came two miles all over the tiles,
As gaily as if for a marriage;
But Green-eye O'Gride and...tortoiseshell bride
Drove up to the door in...carriage.
How the people all stared!...he dogs all declared
They never saw handsomer carriage.

WARNE'S PICTURE PUZZ... TOY BOO... THE HO... WE LIVE...

LONDON, F. WARNE...

ALICE'S ADVENTURES IN WONDERLAND.

BY LEWIS CARROLL.

WITH FORTY-TWO ILLUSTRATIONS BY JOHN TENNIEL.

EIGHTH THOUSAND.

London: MACMILLAN AN... 1867.

THROUGH THE LOOKING-GLASS,

AND WHAT ALICE FOUND THERE.

BY LEWIS CARROLL.

WITH FIFTY ILLUSTRATIONS BY JOHN TENNIEL.

London: MACMILLAN AND CO 1872.

With the arrival of cheaper methods of colour printing during the 1860s and after, a profusion of decorative illustrated books for fortunate children were now available; prior to this many books had been hand coloured, such as the Struwwelpeter book on p. 40/41. Dean's movable books were a novelty providing animated pictures for such titles as Pussy's Party (above) published in 1860. Lewis Carroll's classics Alice's Adventures in Wonderland (1865) and Through the Looking-Glass (1871) were illustrated by John Tenniel. Other great children's book artists included Walter Crane, whose Baby's Opera (1877) and Baby's Bouquet (1878) were both mass produced; Randolf Caldecott (Queen of Hearts, 1881, The Milkmaid, 1882, and The Three Jovial Huntsmen, 1880), and Kate Greenaway who came to prominence in the 1880s with such titles as A Apple Pie (1886). In 1895 Florence Upton created a 'golliwogg' for her first book.

See pages 36-37

Beyond the traditional children's books, there existed a wide range of children's periodicals, from the hard bound annual to weekly papers and flimsy story books (often known as 'bloods') that flourished in the 1880s and '90s.

Pre-eminent was The Boy's Own Paper launched in 1879. The halfpenny comics arrived in the 1890s (see p.3).

The Queen... He...

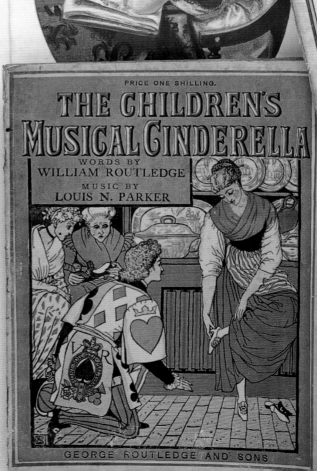

PRICE ONE SHILLING.

THE CHILDREN'S MUSICAL CINDERELLA

WORDS BY WILLIAM ROUTLEDGE
MUSIC BY LOUIS N. PARKER

GEORGE ROUTLEDGE AND SONS

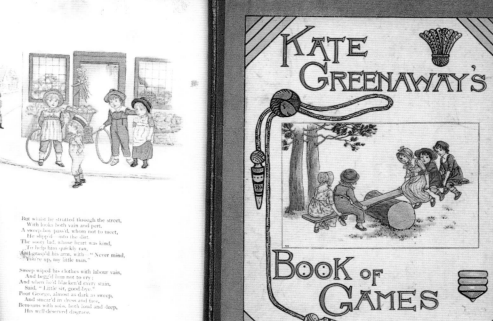

Just when he strutted through the street,
With looks both vain and pert,
A sweep has pass'd, whom not to meet,
He slipp'd—into the dirt.

The sooty lad, whose heart was kind,
To help him quickly ran,
And grasp'd his arm, with " Never mind,
You're up, my little man."

Sweep wiped his clothes with labour vain,
And begg'd him not to cry;
And when he'd blacken'd every stain,
Said, " Little sir, good-bye."

Poor George, almost as dark as sweep,
And smear'd in dress and face,
Bemoans with woe, both loud and deep,
His well-deserved disgrace.

N NODDED FOR IT

KATE GREENAWAY'S
BOOK of GAMES
GEORGE ROUTLEDGE & SONS

THE BABY'S OPERA

A·BOOK·OF·OLD·RHYMES·WITH·NEW·DRESSES
BY WALTER·CRANE
THE·MUSIC·BY·THE·EARLIEST·MASTERS

If you have no daugh-ters, If you have no daugh-ters, if you have no

daugh-ters, Pray give them to your sons!

those lit-tle-ones, Then you must eat them all your-selves.

THE BABY'S BOUQUET
A COMPANION TO THE BABY'S OPERA
A FRESH BUNCH OF OLD RHYMES & TUNES
ARRANGED & DECORATED BY WALTER·CRANE

THE ADVENTURES of two DUTCH DOLLS
BY FLORENCE K. UPTON

Words by BERTHA UPTON

LONGMANS GREEN & CO, LONDON & NEW YORK

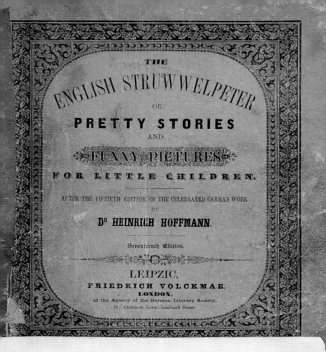

THE
ENGLISH STRUWWELPETER
OR
PRETTY STORIES
AND
FUNNY PICTURES
FOR LITTLE CHILDREN.

AFTER THE FIFTIETH EDITION OF THE CELEBRATED GERMAN WORK
OF
Dr HEINRICH HOFFMANN.

Seventeenth Edition.

LEIPZIC,
FRIEDRICH VOLCKMAR.
LONDON.
at the Agency of the German Literary Society,
37, Abchurch Lane, Lombard Street.

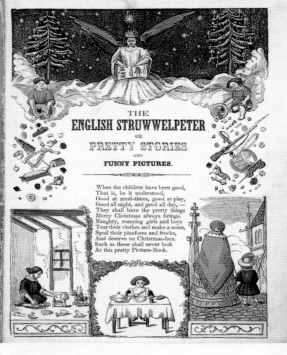

THE
ENGLISH STRUWWELPETER
OR
PRETTY STORIES
AND
FUNNY PICTURES.

When the children have been good,
That is, be it understood,
Good at meal-times, good at play,
Good all night, and good all day,—
They shall have the pretty things
Merry Christmas always brings.
Naughty, romping girls and boys,
Tear their clothes and make a noise,
Spoil their pinafores and frocks,
And deserve no Christmas-box.
Such as these shall never look
At this pretty Picture-Book.

1. SHOCK-HEADED PETER.

Just look at him! There he stands,
With his nasty hair and hands.
See! his nails are never cut;
They are grim'd as black as soot;
And the sloven, I declare,
Never once has comb'd his hair;
Any thing to me is sweeter
Than to see Shock-headed Peter.
(2)

3. THE DREADFUL STORY ABOUT HARRIET AND THE MATCHES.

It almost makes me cry to tell
What foolish Harriet befell.
Mamma and Nurse went out one day,
And left her all alone at play;
Now, on the table close at hand,
A box of matches chanc'd to stand;
And kind Mamma and Nurse had told her,
That if she touch'd them, they should scold her
But Harriet said, "Oh, what a pity!
For, when they burn, it is so pretty;
They crackle so, and spit, and flame;
Mamma, too, often does the same."

The pussy-cats heard this,
And they began to hiss,
And stretch their claws,
And raise their paws;
"Me-ow," they said, "me-ow, me-o,
You'll burn to death, if you do so".

But Harriet would not take advice,
She lit a match, it was so nice!
It crackled so, it burn'd so clear,—
Exactly like the picture here.
She jump'd for joy and ran about,
And was too pleas'd to put it out.

The pussy-cats saw this,
And said, "Oh, naughty, naughty Miss!"
And stretch'd their claws,
And rais'd their paws;
"'Tis very, very wrong, you know,
Me-ow, me-o, me-ow, me-o,
You will be burnt, if you do so".

And see! Oh! what a dreadful thing!
The fire has caught her apron-string;
Her apron burns, her arms, her hair;
She burns all over, every where.

Then how the pussy-cats did mew,
What else, poor pussies, could they do?
They scream'd for help, 'twas all in vain!
So then, they said, "we'll scream again;
Make haste, make haste, me-ow, me-o,
She'll burn to death, we told her so."

So she was burnt, with all her clothes,
And arms, and hands, and eyes and nose;
Till she had nothing more to lose
Except her little scarlet shoes;
And nothing else but these was found
Among her ashes on the ground.

And when the good cats sat beside
The smoking ashes, how they cried!
"Me-ow, me-o, me-ow, me-o,
What will Mamma and Nursy do?"
Their tears ran down their cheeks so fast;
They made a little pond at last.

4. THE STORY OF THE INKY BOYS.

As he had often done before,
The woolly-headed black-a-moor
One nice fine summer's day went out
To see the shops and walk about;
And as he found it hot, poor fellow,
He took with him his green umbrella.
Then Edward, little noisy wag,
Ran out and laugh'd, and wav'd his flag;
And William came in jacket trim,
And brought his wooden hoop with him;
And Arthur, too, snatch'd up his toys
And join'd the other naughty boys;
So, one and all set up a roar
And kept on singing,— only think!
"Oh! Blacky, you're as black as ink."

5. THE STORY OF THE MAN THAT WENT OUT SHOOTING.

This is the man that shoots the hares;
This is the coat he always wears:
With game-bag, powder-horn and gun,
He's going out to have some fun.

He finds it hard, without a pair
Of spectacles, to shoot the hare.

The hare sits snug in leaves and grass,
And laughs to see the green man pass.

Now, as the sun grew very hot,
And he a heavy gun had got,
He lay down underneath a tree
And went to sleep, as you may see;
And, while he slept like any top,
The little hare came, hop, hop, hop,—
Took gun and spectacles, and then
On her hind legs went off again.

The green man wakes and sees her place
The spectacles upon her face;
And now she's trying, all she can,
To shoot the sleepy green-coat man.
He cries and screams and runs away;
The hare runs after him all day,
And hears him call out every where,
"Help! Fire! Help! The Hare! The Hare!"

At last he stumbled at the well
Head over ears, and in he fell.
The hare stopp'd short, took aim, and hark!
Bang went the gun,— she miss'd her mark!

The poor man's wife was drinking up
Her coffee in her coffee-cup;
The gun shot cup and saucer through;
"O dear!" cried she, "what shall I do?"
There liv'd close by the cottage there
The hare's own child, the little hare;
And while she stood upon her toes,
The coffee fell and burn'd her nose.
"O dear!" she cried, with spoon in hand,
"Such fun I do not understand."

8. THE STORY OF FIDGETY PHILIP

Let me see if Philip can
Be a little gentleman;
Let me see, if he is able
To sit still for once at table:
Thus Papa bade Phil behave;
And Mamma look'd very grave.
But fidgety Phil,
He won't sit still;
He wriggles
And giggles,
And then, I declare,
Swings backwards and forwards
And tilts up his chair,
Just like any rocking horse;—
"Philip! I am getting cross!"

See the naughty restless child
Growing still more rude and wild,
Till his chair falls over quite.
Philip screams with all his might,
Catches at the cloth, but then
That makes matters worse again.
Down upon the ground they fall,
Glasses, plates, knives, forks and all.
How Mamma did fret and frown,
When she saw them tumbling down!
And Papa made such a face!
Philip is in sad disgrace.

Where is Philip, where is he?
Fairly cover'd up you see!
Cloth and all are lying on him;
He has pull'd down all upon him.
What a terrible to-do!
Dishes, glasses, snapt in two!
Here a knife, and there a fork!
Philip, this is cruel work.
Table all so bare, and ah!
Poor Papa, and poor Mamma
Look quite cross, and wonder how
They shall make their dinner now.

9. THE STORY OF

As he trudg'd along to school,
It was always Johnny's rule
To be looking at the sky
And the clouds that floated by;
But what just before him lay,
In his way,
Johnny never thought about;
So that every one cried out
"Look at little Johnny there,
Little Johnny Head-In-Air."

Running just in Johnny's way,
Came a little dog one day;
Johnny's eyes were still astray
Up on high,
In the sky;
And he never heard them cry
"Johnny, mind, the dog is nigh!"
Bump!
Dump!
Down they fell, with such a thump,
Dog and Johnny in a lump!

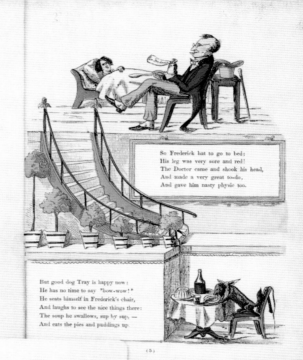

The trough was full, and faithful Tray
Came out to drink one sultry day;
He wagg'd his tail, and wet his lip,
When cruel Fred snatch'd up a whip,
And whipp'd poor Tray till he was sore,
And kick'd and whipp'd him more and more;
At this, good Tray grew very red,
And growl'd and bit him till he bled;
Then you should only have been by,
To see how Fred did scream and cry!

So Frederick had to go to bed;
His leg was very sore and red;
The Doctor came and shook his head,
And made a very great to-do,
And gave him nasty physic too.

But good dog Tray is happy now:
He has no time to say "bow-wow."
He seats himself in Frederick's chair,
And laughs to see the nice things there:
The soup he swallows, sup by sup,—
And eats the pies and puddings up.

Now tall Agrippa lived close by, —
So tall, he almost touch'd the sky;
He had a mighty inkstand too,
In which a great goose-feather grew;
He call'd out in an angry tone,
"Boys, leave the black-a-moor alone!
For if he tries with all his might,
He cannot change from black to white."
But ah! they did not mind a bit
What great Agrippa said of it;
But went on laughing, as before,
And hooting at the black-a-moor.

Then great Agrippa foams with rage,
Look at him on this very page!
He seizes Arthur, seizes Ned,
Takes William by his little head;

And they may scream and kick and call,
Into the ink he dips them all;
Into the inkstand, one, two, three,
Till they are black, as black can be;
Turn over now and you shall see.

See, there they are, and there they ran!
The black-a-moor enjoys the fun.
They have been made as black as crows,
Quite black all over, eyes and nose,
And trowsers, pinafores and toys,
The silly little inky boys!
Because they set up such a roar,
And teas'd the harmless black-a-moor.

7. THE STORY OF AUGUSTUS WHO WOULD NOT HAVE ANY SOUP.

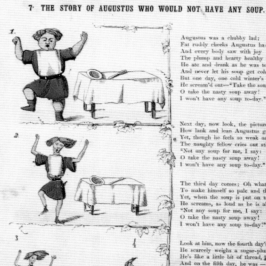

Augustus was a chubby lad;
Fat ruddy cheeks Augustus had;
And every body saw with joy
The plump and hearty healthy boy.
He ate and drank as he was told,
And never let his soup get cold.
But one day, one cold winter's day,
He scream'd out—"Take the soup away!
O take the nasty soup away!
I won't have any soup to-day."

Next day, now look, the picture shows
How lank and lean Augustus grows!
Yet, though he feels so weak and ill,
The naughty fellow cries out still—
"Not any soup for me, I say:
O take the nasty soup away!
I won't have any soup to-day."

The third day comes; Oh what a sin!
To make himself so pale and thin.
Yet, when the soup is put on table,
He screams, as loud as he is able,—
"Not any soup for me, I say:
O take the nasty soup away!
I won't have any soup to-day."

Look at him, now the fourth day's come!
He scarcely weighs a sugar-plum;
He's like a little bit of thread,
And on the fifth day, he was—dead!

6. THE STORY OF LITTLE SUK-A-THUMB.

One day, Mamma said: "Conrad dear,
I must go out and leave you here.
But mind now, Conrad, what I say,
Don't suck your thumb while I'm away.
The great tall tailor always comes
To little boys that suck their thumbs;
And ere they dream what he's about,
He takes his great sharp scissars out
And cuts their thumbs clean off, — and then,
You know, they never grow again."

Mamma had scarcely turn'd her back,
The thumb was in, Alack! Alack!

The door flew open, in he ran,
The great, long, red-legg'd scissar-man.
Oh! children, see! the tailor's come
And caught out little Suck-a-Thumb.
Snip! Snap! Snip! the scissars go;
And Conrad cries out — Oh! Oh! Oh!
Snip! Snap! Snip! They go so fast;
That both his thumbs are off at last.

Mamma comes home; there Conrad stands,
And looks quite sad, and shows his hands; —
"Ah!" said Mamma, "I knew he'd come
To naughty little Suck-a-Thumb."

Once, with head as high as ever,
Johnny walk'd beside the river.
Johnny watch'd the swallows trying
Which was cleverest at flying.
Oh! what fun!
Johnny watch'd the bright round sun
Going in and coming out;
This was all he thought about.
So he strode on, only think!
To the river's very brink,
Where the bank was high and steep,
And the water very deep;
And the fishes, in a row,
Stared to see him coming so.

One step more! Oh! sad to tell!
Headlong in poor Johnny fell.
And the fishes, in dismay,
Wagg'd their tails and ran away.

There lay Johnny on his face,
With his nice red writing-case;
But, as they were passing by,
Two strong men had heard him cry;
And, with sticks, these two strong men
Hook'd poor Johnny out again.

Oh! you should have seen him shiver
When they pull'd him from the river.
He was in a sorry plight,
Dripping wet, and such a fright!
Wet all over, every where,
Clothes and arms and face and hair;
Johnny never will forget
What it is to be so wet.

And the fishes, one, two, three,
Are come back again, you see;
Up they came the moment after,
To enjoy the fun and laughter.
Each popp'd out his little head,
And, to tease poor Johnny, said
"Silly Johnny, look,
You have lost your writing-book!"

10. THE STORY OF FLYING ROBERT.

When the rain comes tumbling down
In the country or the town,
All good little girls and boys
Stay at home and mind their toys.
Robert thought, — "No, when it pours,
It is better out of doors."
Rain it did, and in a minute
Bob was in it.
Here you see him, silly fellow,
Underneath his red umbrella.

What a wind! Oh! how it whistles
Through the trees and flow'rs and thistles!
It has caught his red umbrella;
Now look at him, silly fellow,
Up he flies
To the skies.
No one heard his screams and cries;
Through the clouds the rude wind bore him,
And his hat flew on before him.

Soon they got to such a height,
They were nearly out of sight!
And the last wont up so high,
That it really touch'd the sky.
No one ever yet could tell
Where they stopp'd, or where they fell:
Only, this one thing is plain,
Bob was never seen again!

All the moral values of Victorian society were embodied in Struwwelpeter, a book first published in 1845 in Germany. This book of cautionary tales was translated into English in 1848, becoming immensely popular. This seventeenth edition with hand-coloured illustrations dates from around 1870. Each of the ten tales dwelt on some misdemeanour - table manners, sucking thumbs or the misuse of matches (a new invention when this book first came out).

Established 1856
PROSSER & SONS
Lawn Tennis Racket & Ball.

CROQUET SCHOTTISCHE.

PLAY UP CARDIFF

ROCHDALE

BOLTON WANDERERS PLAY UP

WANDERE

WELL PLAYED

SALFORD

BRIGHOUSE RANGERS

WIGAN

LONDON SCOTTISH

STICK TO HIM

SHEFFIELD UNITED ASSOCIATION FOOTBALL TEAM

FOOTBALL;
OR,
MISERY AND MUD.

Written by
WAL PINK,

Compos
W. G. F

F. H. AYRES'

MANUFACTURER OF
Sports & Games
111, ALDERSGATE ST. LONDON.

SUNLIGHT YEAR BOOKS, 1895
SPORTS

LEVER BROTHERS L?
PORT SUNLIGHT.

"The People's" SPORTIN

E. D. BROWN   W. L. HOLLICK   E. W. HAYDEN   A. P

VAMPIRES' FOOTBALL CLUB

HALIFAX

Manningham

As the urbanisation of Britain developed, many sports needed standard rules that enabled teams to compete on equal terms. The Football Association was founded in 1863 and the Rugby Football Union in 1871. Modern croquet had been introduced in 1857, with the first championship ten years later; however, lawn tennis overtook it as the most popular social game. Tennis rules were standardised in 1874 and the first championship was held at Wimbledon in 1877. While the origins of cricket can be traced back to the Midde Ages, and the Marylebone Cricket Club to 1787, the composition cricket ball was patented in 1860 and the first test match, between England and Australia, was played in 1877. WG Grace played first class cricket between 1865 and 1900. The first British Open golf championship was played in 1860. Polo was introduced from India in 1869.

P. R. HARROWER   T. SNOWDEN   G. J. GROVES, Captain

The Song of the CYCLIST

Dedicated to R. Cameron Esqre Junr L.B.C.
President of the Monstre Meet, Liverpool

Beeston's GLOBE CYCLE CO. Ltd.
GREEN LANE, WOLVERHAMPTON.
SEASON 1899

WINGYCLES
WHITE MACHINE Co.
48. HOLBORN VIA. LONDON
1898

LEA CYCLES
Lea & Francis Ltd
COVENTRY

"The ÉLITE" GAITERS
MAX FRANKENBURG'S PATENT

THE "ÉLITE" GAITERS
with the Patent
Application enhances the fit,
gives ease & comfort to the wearer

WHEN BUYING ASK FOR THE "ÉLITE"

ECLIPSE BICYCLE
They Stand The Test

SPECIALITÉ
THE CYCLE BISCUIT,
Highly Nitrogenous & Digestive
CYCLISTS
MEREDITH WATER & DREW Ltd

HUNTLEY & PALMERS BISCUITS
READING & LONDON

Mc Vitie & Price's
Cyclist Biscuits.
RALEIGH

THE "ARIEL" BICYCLE.

all about Dunlop Tyres
for 1896

BARTLETT CLINCHER TYRE
FIRST · DETACHABLE · PNEUMATIC · TYRE INVENTED
INTRODUCED in 1890
ADOPTED BY H.M. Post Office.

Fitted with Lever Tension Wheels, India Rubber Tyres, Improved Rudder, Registered Clippet Sliding Spring, &c.

TARLEY & COMPANY
PATENTEES & MANUFACTURERS.
ST. AGNES WORKS, COVENTRY

This Song may be Sung in Public without fee or Licence Except at Theatres & Music Halls

MARIE LLOYD'S LATEST SUCCESS
SALUTE MY BICYCLE

CHORUS
The fellows all "chike"
When they see me on my 'bike'
But I'm as cool as any icicle;
They can chaff me all they like,
But I never get the 'spike'
I only say, Salute my bicycle!

SHEET NO. 3.
BACON'S Cycling Road-Map OF ENGLAND
In Seven Sheets, with the Main Roads Specially Coloured.
Prices - In Case, 1/-. On Flexible Cloth, 2/6. On Cloth, cut to fold, 3/6.
LONDON: G. W. BACON & CO., 127, STRAND.

Cycling became fashionable during the 1870s
when the bone shaker was replaced by the 'ordinary'
bicycle, such as the Ariel bicycle of 1872 (above).
The 'ordinary' bicycles were known affectionately
by the 1890s as 'penny farthings' after the 'safety'
cycle had replaced them from 1882 onwards. Easier
to maintain than a horse, the bicycle represented not
only novelty, but a new independence. The demand
for road maps increased. Other leisure pursuits included
roller skating or 'rinking' (the craze starting in the 1870s),
the theatre and going to exhibitions such as those
held at Olympia and Earls Court, where the
Big Wheel was built in 1895.

44

Well before the end of the century the railway network had opened up the seaside resorts to most of the population, while steamships provided more convenient access to the new world of America and to the Mediterranean ports. Cooks tourist excursions had started in 1841; and by the 1890s travellers could purchase 'hotel coupons' to pre-pay accommodation. Tit-Bits guide to Paris of 1889 included details of the Paris Universal Exhibition and the newly-built Eiffel Tower. Blackpool's tower was built in 1894, and its lettered rock was the first to be sold, in 1876.

46

THE POSTMAN'S KNOCK.

SUNG AT THE THEATRE ROYAL HAYMARKET, BY WILLIAM FARREN ESQ^R, SUNG ALSO AT THE SURREY THEATRE.

SONG

LONDON. ROBERT COCKS & Co NEW BURLINGTON ST. MUSIC PUBLISHERS TO HER MOST GRACIOUS AND HIS IMPERIAL MAJESTY THE EMPEROR NAPOLEON III.

HORNER'S CHRISTMAS NUMBER 1896.

With Coloured Plate

Our Neighbour Over the Way

POST OFFICE TELEGRAPHS.

Regulation as to Inland Telegrams.

If the Receiver of an Inland Message doubts its accuracy, he may have it repeated on paying half the cost of its transmission to him. In the event of an error having been made, the amount paid for repetition will be refunded on application to the Secretary.

POSTAL ORDER FOR TWENTY SHILLINGS

POSTAL ORDER ONE SHILLING 1/-

NOT NEGOTIABLE.

POST CARD

FOREIGN POST CARD
FOR COUNTRIES INCLUDED IN THE POSTAL UNION.

UNION POSTALE UNIVERSELLE
POST CARD—GREAT BRITAIN & IRELAND
(GRANDE BRETAGNE ET IRLANDE)
THE ADDRESS ONLY TO BE WRITTEN ON THIS SIDE.

BOURNEMOUTH.

THE POSTMAN
OR Do like to be in the "Know," you know.

Royal Mail.

POST OFFICE SAVINGS BANK.
GOVERNMENT SECURITY.

THESE PARTICULARS OF ACCOUNT MUST BE GIVEN IN ALL COMMUNICATIONS WITH THE SAVINGS BANK DEPARTMENT

ST. ALBANS

18214

DEPOSITS.

INVESTMENTS IN GOVERNMENT STOCK

IMMEDIATE ANNUITIES
AND
DEFERRED ANNUITIES (OLD AGE PAY)

LIFE INSURANCE.

DEPOSITS.
AN ACCOUNT OF SUMS DEPOSITED BY
Miss Janet Russel

Roland Hill's reforms for the postal system began in May 1840 when the first adhesive stamps came into use – the Penny Black and Twopenny Blue – a flat rate charge to any part of Great Britain. These stamps needed to be cut out with scissors. Then in 1854 the Penny Red was introduced that had perforated edges. Postcards with stamps already printed on them were issued in 1870; pictorial postcards were allowed from 1894. The Post Office Savings Bank began in 1861, the Post Office Telegraph System in 1870 and Postal Orders in 1881. Although Valentine messages had been around since before 1800, they became far more popular once the penny postal service began.

48

A SUGGESTIVE VIEW.
(DESIGNED EXPRESSLY FOR YOU.)

NOTICE
PERSONS ATTEMPTING
TO CROSS THE LINE
RENDER THEMSELVES
LIABLE TO
SEVERE PUNISHMENT

A TRIBUTE TO MY FAIR

Oh, miserable, lonely wretch!
Despised by all who know you;
Haste, haste, your days to end—this sketch
The quickest way will show you!

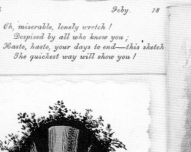

What a jackass you look to be sure,
In spite of your clothing so gay;
Folks very soon will you good day,
For you're stupid and dull as a mule,
Fit only to laugh at and joke.

Cupid throws his Gauntlet down,
Challenging, and all the rest
Never fear his blind'ning frown,
Love his ears, the little pest!

Although in uniform thou lookest nobby,
Oh stern & fierce art thou my bobby.
No servant maid with smile can melt thee.
The boys all hate & sometimes pelt thee
Grim-visaged war once smooth'd his front
But oh its evident you wont

With your Ribbons gay in bright array,
Enough to deck a Queen,
The live-long day you flirt away,
With lots of Crinoline,
But lurking there I do opine
You'll never catch a Valentine

Industrious creature! oh, Penelope Prim,
Dont think by such scheming that you will win him
While pretending to work, from your eye you look out
To see what the belles and the beaux are about.
Malice, envy, and, jealousy lurk in your face,
That makes your sour countenance full of grimace;
Your delight is to break of some happy love-match
From others more handsome than you are, to match
The bliss of existence. False creature, repine,
Think not by such wiles to get a Valentine

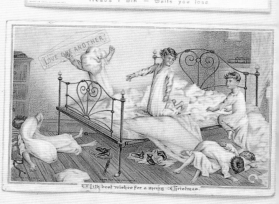

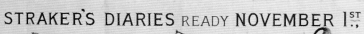

FOR THE
PIANO-FORTE,
FRANÇOIS CLAREN
LONDON, S. J. BREWER & C°.

THE
JOVIAL CHRISTMAS

POLKA.

BY
W. SMALLWOOD

The traditions of Christmas time
were consolidated during Victoria's
reign. Prince Albert had
introduced the German Christmas
tree during the 1840s, and the
sending of Christmas cards
became increasingly popular
from the 1850s onwards, the
designs becoming more exotic
and frivolous. Santa Claus
brought the toys (wearing a
red, blue, brown or grey
coat). Crackers gradually
became part of the
festivities from the 1840s. 51

For Queen Victoria's Jubilee celebrations of 1887 (Golden) and 1897 (Diamond), hundreds of souvenirs were made — so many in fact that one song sheet with Gladstone on the cover lampooned the way in which every type of article had become a Jubilee accessory, from pills to frying pans. Along with the pottery and tin mugs, plates and relief scraps, there were now, in 1897, commemorative postcards – plain or coloured.

Much of Britain's power and prestige was founded on her military prowess. The army and navy had extended and defended the Empire, as well as maintaining a certain order as a world power, for instance in the Afghan War of 1878-81. Heroic deeds were never far away; eight Victoria Crosses were awarded during the battle at Rorke's Drift in 1879 during the Zulu War (the VC was first given in 1856 for valour during the Crimean War). The origins of the Military Tournament date back to 1880 - the booklet opposite of 1900 covers its 21st year at the Agricultural Hall.

After some trouble in South Africa in 1881, Britain recognised the independence of Transvaal. However, fighting with the Boers began again in 1899, leading to the historic sieges of 1900 at Ladysmith and Mafeking. The Boer War finally ended in 1902 making heroes of the generals. The Absent-Minded Beggar was written by Rudyard Kipling soon after the outbreak of war in October 1899 — the proceeds went to the Daily Mail's fund for soldiers' wives and children: the fund raised £250,000.

B.C. 55

THE ROMANS.
JULIUS CÆSAR.
First Invasion by Julius Caesar B.C. 55.
Second landing of the Romans B.C. 54.
Conquest by Claudius Caesar A.D. 43.
London founded.
Resistance of Caractacus.
His capture, and release by Claudius.

A.D. 62

BOADICEA,
QUEEN OF THE ICENI.
The Romans defeated by Boadicea.
Boadicea afterwards defeated by the Romans.
Conquest completed by Agricola, 85.
CONSTANTINE III.
LAST ROMAN SOVEREIGN.
The Romans having introduced civilization,
laws, and the arts of peace, quit Britain 446.

A.D. 450

THE SAXONS.
HENGIST AND HORSA.
Arrival of the Saxons 449.
Battle of Aylesford—Horsa killed.
Kingdom of Kent founded by Hengist.
Ravages of the Saxons.
Great numbers of Britons retire into Wales,
and others emigrate to the Continent.

460 – 827

KENT. BEGAN 455. ENDED 754.
SUSSEX. BEGAN 477. ENDED 754.
WESSEX. BEGAN 521. ENDED 800.
ESSEX. BEGAN 527. ENDED 746.
NORTHUMBERLAND. BEGAN 547. ENDED 792.
EAST ANGLIA. BEGAN 571. ENDED 800.
MERCIA. BEGAN 584. ENDED 626.

THE HEPTARCHY.
Britain divided into seven kingdoms.
From Cerdic, 1st King of Wessex,
the present Royal Family in the female line
are descended.
Reign of the renowned Arthur 508.
Arrival of St. Augustine 596. Danes land 787.

800 – 827

ANGLO-SAXONS.
EGBERT,
KING OF WESSEX.
Becomes sole Monarch of England 827.
Expedition against Wales.
Incursions of the Danes. Sheppey ravaged.
Battle of Charmouth.
Danes and Britons defeated by Egbert.

837

ETHELWOLF,
SON OF EGBERT.
Division of England.
The Danes establish themselves in Sh...
They harry London and Canterbury.
Battles of Wembury, Sandwich, and...
Ethelwolf's pilgrimage to Rome.
Rebellion of Ethelbald.

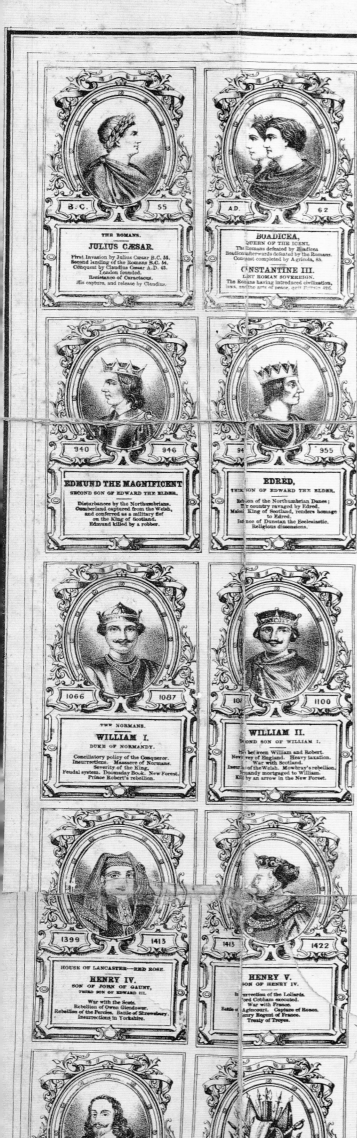

940 – 946

EDMUND THE MAGNIFICENT,
SECOND SON OF EDWARD THE ELDER.
Disturbances by the Northumbrians.
Cumberland captured from the Welsh,
and conferred as a military fief
on the King of Scotland.
Edmund killed by a robber.

946 – 955

EDRED,
THIRD SON OF EDWARD THE ELDER.
Reign of the Northumbrian Danes;
Their country ravaged by Edred.
Malcolm, King of Scotland, renders homage
to Edred.
Influence of Dunstan the Ecclesiastic.
Religious dissensions.

955 – 959

EDWY,
SON OF EDMUND THE MAGNIFICENT.
Disputes with the Monks.
Ill treatment of Queen Elgivi by
Archbishop Odo.
Edwy compelled to divorce the Queen.
Elgiva cruelly murdered.
Rebellion. Edwy excommunicated.

959 – 975

EDGAR,
SECOND SON OF EDMUND.
Forty Benedictine monasteries founded.
A powerful Navy defends the coast.
The Northumbrians and Scots overawed.
Ethelwold's treachery and his assassination.
The King marries Elfrida.
Foreigners encouraged to settle in England.

975 – 978

EDWARD THE MARTYR,
SON OF EDGAR.
Succeeds to the Crown at the age of Fifteen.
To raise her own son to the throne,
The Monks expelled from Mercia.
Edward
murdered by his step-mother Elfrida.

978

ETHELRED II.
SON OF EDGAR.
Landing of Danes, who are bribed to...
Treachery of Alfric, Duke of Mercia.
Invasion of Danes under Sweyn and...
Ethelred marries Emma of Normandy.
Massacre of Danes.
Further invasions. Flight of Ethe...

1066 – 1087

THE NORMANS.
WILLIAM I.
DUKE OF NORMANDY.
Conciliatory policy of the Conqueror.
Insurrections. Massacre of Normans.
Severity of the King.
Feudal system. Doomsday Book. New Forest.
Prince Robert's rebellion.

1087 – 1100

WILLIAM II.
SECOND SON OF WILLIAM I.
War between William and Robert.
New levy of England. Heavy taxation.
War with Scotland.
Insurrection of the Welsh. Mowbray's rebellion.
Normandy mortgaged to William.
Killed by an arrow in the New Forest.

1100 – 1135

HENRY I.
THIRD SON OF WILLIAM I.
Seizes the throne in the absence of his
older brother Robert.
Conciliates the nobles by a charter.
Invasion of Normandy.
Disputes with the Pope. War with France.
Prince William drowned at sea.

1135 – 1154

HOUSE OF BLOIS.
STEPHEN,
SON OF ADELA, DAUGHTER OF WM. I.
Usurps the throne. Opposition of Matilda.
Civil Wars. Battle of the Standard.
Confusion and misery in England.
Invasion of Prince Henry, son of Matilda.
Power, fall, and death of Matilda.
Treaty of Winchester.

1154 – 1189

HOUSE OF PLANTAGENET.
HENRY II.
SON OF MATILDA, DAUGHTER OF WM. I.
Peace and security restored.
War with the Welsh, and with France.
Constitutions of Clarendon.
Power, fall, and death of Becket.
Conquest of Ireland. Rebellion of Henry's sons.

1189

RICHARD I.
SECOND SON OF HENRY II.
Persecution of the Jews.
Oppressive exactions of the King.
Richard departs on the Crusade.
Disorders in England.
Capture and ransom of Richard.
War with France.

1399 – 1413

HOUSE OF LANCASTER—RED ROSE.
HENRY IV.
SON OF JOHN OF GAUNT,
THIRD SON OF EDWARD III.
War with the Scots.
Rebellion of Owen Glendower.
Rebellion of the Percies. Battle of Shrewsbury.
Insurrections in Yorkshire.

1413 – 1422

HENRY V.
SON OF HENRY IV.
Insurrection of the Lollards.
Lord Cobham executed.
War with France.
Battle of Agincourt. Capture of Rouen.
Henry Regent of France.
Treaty of Troyes.

1422 – 1461

HENRY VI.
SON OF HENRY V.
Succeeds at the age of Nine Months.
Exploits of Joan of Arc.
Normandy lost. Jack Cade's rebellion.
Wars of the Roses begun.
Edward of York assumes the Crown.

1461 – 1483

HOUSE OF YORK—WHITE ROSE.
EDWARD IV.
Wars of the Roses continued.
Henry and Edward, both prisoners.
Power of the Earl of Warwick.
Henry restored 1470, dies 1471.
Duke of Clarence murdered.
Printing by Caxton.

1483 – 1483

EDWARD V.
SON OF EDWARD IV.
Succeeds at the age of Thirteen.
Richard Duke of Gloster, Regent.
The King's relations arrested.
Lord Hastings beheaded.
Penance of Jane Shore.
Gloster aims at the Crown.

1483

RICHARD III.
BROTHER OF EDWARD IV.
Assumes the Crown.
Murders the two young Princes
in the Tower.
Duke of Buckingham executed.
Invasion by Henry Earl of Richmond.
Battle of Bosworth, Richard slain.

1625 – 1649

CHARLES I.
SON OF JAMES I.
Trial and execution of Strafford.
Rebellion in Ireland.
Disputes with the Parliament.
Civil War.
Archbishop Laud and Hampden beheaded.
The King tried and beheaded.

1649 – 1660

THE COMMONWEALTH.
Cromwell Lord Protector.
The Scots defeated at Dunbar.
Battle of Worcester, 1651.
Scotland admitted into England.
Dutch War. Exploits of Blake.
Cromwell dissolves the Long Parliament.
Prince Charles lands at Dover, 1660.

1660 – 1685

CHARLES II.
SECOND SON OF CHARLES I.
Restored by General Monk.
Naval victories over the Dutch.
Plague in London. Great Fire.
Impeachment of Clarendon.
Habeas Corpus Act. Rye House Plot.
Russell and Sydney beheaded.

1685 – 1688

JAMES II.
SECOND SON OF CHARLES I.
Monmouth's rebellion.
Battle of Sedgemoor, Monmouth defeated.
Disputes with the Bishops.
Descendant of the people.
Prince of Orange invited over.
Revolution.

1689 – 1702

WILLIAM III.
GRANDSON OF CHARLES I.
MARRIED TO MARY, DAUGH. OF JAMES II.
War with France.
Battle of the Boyne. Siege of Limerick.
Death of Queen Mary, 1694.
Battle of La Hogue. Dieppe bombarded.
Peace of Ryswick.
War of the Spanish succession.

1702

ANNE,
DAUGHTER OF JAMES II.
Gibraltar and Guadaloupe taken.
Marlborough's victories.
Battles of Blenheim and Ramillies.
Union of England and Scotland.
Lisle and Tournay taken.
Treaty of Utrecht.

Drawn & Lithographed by ... Hatton Garden. Published ...